Remarkable Landmarks

Our Rocky Mountains

by Dani Neiley

Consultant

Cheryl Lane, M.Ed.
Classroom Teacher, California

Publishing Credits

Rachelle Cracchiolo, M.S.Ed., *Publisher*
Emily R. Smith, M.A.Ed., *SVP of Content Development*
Véronique Bos, *VP of Creative*
Dona Rice, *Senior Content Manager*
Tyler Maynard, *Graphic Designer*

Image Credits: p.8 (left) Adobe Photoshop AI Image Generator; p.8 (right) Alamy/Pictorial Press Ltd; p.9 (top) Library of Congress [LOC-LC-USZ62-32996] ; p.9 (bottom) Library of Congress [LOC-LC-USZ62-101036]; p.11 Adobe Firefly AI Image Generator p.16 (bottom left) Library of Congress [LOC-LC-USZ62-111566]; p.16 (bottom right) Alamy/Marilyn Angel Wynn; p.20 Public Domain; p.22 (bottom) Alamy/The History Collection; all other images from iStock, Shutterstock, and/or in the public domain

This book has been filed with the Library of Congress.
LCCN: 2026018290
ISBN: 979-8-3309-2995-5

TCM Teacher Created Materials
5482 Argosy Avenue
Huntington Beach, CA 92649
www.tcmpub.com

Printed by 51250
PO 22957 / Printed in USA

Table of Contents

How Can Landmarks Shape the Culture of an Area? 2

Welcome to the Rockies! 4

The Rockies Through Time 8

From Rocks to Rockies 10

People of the Rockies 16

See You in the Rockies! 22

Around the World 24

Just for You 26

Glossary 28

Index 29

Be Curious 30

About the Author 30

How Can Landmarks Shape the Culture of an Area?

Landmarks are *all around us!* These special places show us the beauty in our world. They also tell the story of a place and the people who live there. Human-made landmarks, such as statues or temples, can show what a community values most. Natural landmarks, such as mountain ranges and rivers, can inspire local art, music, or traditions.

Think about the places you've been. What landmarks have you seen, and how do they affect the way people live, work, and celebrate?

Pyramids of Giza, Egypt

Matterhorn, Switzerland

Mountain of Seven Colors

Vinicunca is a mountain in Peru. It is also called "Rainbow Mountain." Can you see why? Different minerals cause the colorful stripes. For example, iron makes some rocks red and orange.

Black Canyon of the Gunnison, Colorado

What makes the Rocky Mountains so remarkable?

Let's find out!

Welcome to the Rockies!

Cold wind breezes past you, filling the air with the sharp smell of pine trees. Tall, rocky cliffs rise high into the sky. An eagle soars above you, and a chipmunk scampers across a log. Pine needles **crunch** and **scatter** under your hiking boots.

Welcome to the Rocky Mountains!

Rocky Mountain bighorn sheep

For thousands of years, people have been drawn to the Rockies. The mountains have many natural **resources**, unique plants and animals, and plenty of opportunities to explore. They are more than 3,000 miles (4,800 kilometers) long and reach more than 2.5 miles (4 kilometers) in **elevation**! They are so long they **stretch** through Canada *and* the United States.

Today, these mighty mountains stand out as a symbol of beauty and discovery. They inspire visitors and **locals** alike. They remind everyone of the power of nature.

The Flow of Water

The Continental Divide is found in the Rockies. This is a ridge along the highest peaks. It separates the flow of water in the United States. One side falls to the east and one side to the west.

Rocky Mountain Map

The Rockies are massive! They include more than 100 separate mountain ranges, which can be grouped into four main sections.

Arctic Rockies

- made up of several different mountain ranges
- most **remote** and hardest part of the Rockies to get to

Northern Rockies

- also known as the Canadian Rockies
- more than 2,000 **glaciers** are here

Middle Rockies

- three national parks are here
- known for hot springs, wide valleys, and active geysers

Southern Rockies

- the section of the Rockies with the most elevation
- has the highest peak in the Rockies, Mount Elbert, at 14,431 feet (4,399 meters)

The Rockies Through Time

The Rocky Mountains have been changing for thousands of years. From the first peoples who called them home to the people who live there today, they tell a story of growth and discovery.

10,000–13,500 years ago

Paleo-Indian hunters move into the Rockies after the glaciers melt, following animal herds.

Early to mid-1800s

Settlers begin moving into the Rockies, following the trails of the Indigenous peoples.

3,000–10,000 years ago

Indigenous peoples build thriving communities in the Rockies.

1869

Railroad workers build new train lines in western Wyoming, making travel through the Rockies faster and easier.

1900s

First Nations in Canada and American Indians in the United States continue to honor and protect their **sacred** connection to the mountains.

1904

The Cripple Creek mining boom ends in Colorado. It is the last major gold rush in the Rockies.

1938

Trail Ridge Road in Rocky Mountain National Park is fully completed. It becomes the highest continuous paved road in the United States.

Today

People from around the world live in and visit the Rockies to ski, hike, and enjoy the beauty of these timeless mountains.

From Rocks to Rockies

The story of the Rockies begins about 75 million years ago. That's because it takes a lot of time—and pressure—for mountains to form.

Long ago, pressure began to build up underground. Huge pieces of land and rocks→**pushed against**←each other. They had nowhere to go but *UP!*↑ The pressure brought them to Earth's surface, forming the Rocky Mountains.

Water Power!

Imagine that you're building a sandcastle. An ocean wave surprises you and washes away part of your castle. That's erosion in action!

Over millions of years, the land continued to change. Natural forces shaped the mountains through **erosion**. Wind, rain, and snow wore down the rocks. Icy glaciers carved deep valleys and canyons.

Even today, the Rocky Mountains are a work in progress. The forces of erosion continue to shape the mountains every year.

As the Rockies formed, so did remarkable landscapes. To keep these areas safe and protected, national parks were created. Here are a few you won't want to miss!

Canadian National Parks

Banff National Park is Canada's first national park. It's filled with amazing sights, and Moraine Lake is one of them. This lake is well-known for its **turquoise** water.

Farther north, you'll find Jasper National Park. This is the largest park in the Canadian Rockies. It's known for its hiking trails and wildlife. Bears, moose, bighorn sheep, and more live there.

U.S. National Parks

Geysers and bison are commonly seen in Yellowstone National Park. You'll also find colorful hot springs and learn lots of history in the first U.S. national park.

To the north and south, Glacier and Rocky Mountain National Parks have **scenic** roads. Going-to-the-Sun Road and Trail Ridge Road offer jaw-dropping views of the mountains.

Parks Among the Peaks

Across Canada and the United States, the Rockies are home to ten national parks.

Canada
Jasper
Banff
Yoho
Kootenay
Waterton Lakes

United States
Glacier
Yellowstone
Grand Teton
Rocky Mountain
Black Canyon of the Gunnison

Yellowstone National Park

Ecosystems of the Rockies

Different **ecosystems** exist across the Rockies. Each one has its own plants, animals, and weather. These ecosystems make the Rockies rich and diverse.

Most of the Rockies are made up of forests. Tall pine, fir, and aspen trees can be found here. Animals such as deer, bears, elk, and moose live among the trees. The weather changes with the seasons. Typically, it is WARM in the late spring and summer. The rest of the year is COLD and snowy.

Some parts of the Rockies are known as alpine tundra, meaning that no trees grow above a certain elevation. That's why many peaks in the Rockies have sheer, bare rocks. Mountain goats, marmots, and pikas thrive in these places. The weather is cold most of the year, and some areas have ice or snow year-round. In the short summers, small, **hardy** plants grow, and animals are more active.

Rocky Mountain Ranches

Ranches are a common sight in the valleys of the Rockies. These large, grassy areas are great for raising livestock. You'll see cattle, horses, and sheep on ranches.

People of the Rockies

The Rockies have long been an important place for Indigenous peoples. They have lived there for more than 10,000 years!

United States: American Indians

American Indians have lived and moved through the Rockies for a long time. Some key nations include the Ute, Shoshone, Dakota, and Nimiipuu. These nations once hunted and gathered what they needed. They moved across the land, guided by the seasons. In the summer and fall, they lived high in the mountains. In the winter, they left for the plains.

Today, some nations live in towns and cities in or near the Rockies. Others live on **reservations**. The Rockies remain sacred to American Indians.

1899

Today

Canada: First Nations

In Canada, many Indigenous groups lived and traveled through the Rockies, and some still do. Some key groups include the Stoney Nakoda, Blackfoot Confederacy, and Métis. These groups once had trading centers. The areas that make up Canada's national parks were their meeting places. They used **rivers** to travel distances. The rivers were also good for hunting and fishing.

Today, the Rockies remain sacred to the First Nations. They have always had a strong connection with the land and nature.

The Power of Storytelling

Storytelling is an important part of life for the Stoney Nakoda First Nation. It is a way of teaching and learning. Stories tell of the powers of Lake Minnewanka and explain the **northern lights**, or Aurora Borealis.

Developing the Rockies

In the 1800s, settlers began moving into the Rockies. They wanted to explore, find new opportunities, and build places to call home.

Before long, settlers discovered that the Rockies were full of valuable resources. Animals such as beavers, bison, and rabbits were hunted for their furs. Trees were cut down to build houses. And miners struck gold in the Rockies—literally! Gold rushes took place across the mountain range. Miners also found silver and other **heavy metals** hidden in the rock.

Ghost Towns

Several old mining towns—now ghost towns—can be found in the Rockies. No (or very few) people live there today.

Traveling through the Rockies wasn't easy at first. Wagons had to bump along rough, rocky trails. Trips took a **very long** time. But travel slowly improved. By the 1880s, railroads wound their way through the mountains. Trains carried gold and silver out of the Rockies and brought visitors in to see the stunning views. In the early 1900s, paved roads made it even easier to travel. Before long, anyone with a car could easily head into the Rockies for an adventure!

Tough Travel!

What was it like to travel between towns in the 1890s? Let's look at an example! This bridge was used by people traveling between the towns of Ouray and Silverton in Colorado.

This is a stagecoach, or a wagon with wooden wheels. People used stagecoaches to travel before the invention of cars.

A stagecoach usually had four or six horses at the front. The horses traveled about 10 miles (16 kilometers) at a time. Then, those horses were swapped for new ones when they got tired.

Roads like these were called “stage lines.” These trails were made for stagecoach travel.

In the past, carefully stacked logs were used to build bridges. You might have had to pack some extra bravery to travel across this rickety bridge!

See You in the Rockies!

People come from all over the world to visit the Rocky Mountains. And it's not hard to see why! Every season brings something new to see and do. In the winter and spring, people chase the thrill of skiing down snowy slopes. In the fall, they come to see the leaves turn brilliant colors. And whether there's RAIN, snow, or SUNSHINE, you're sure to find hikers on every trail.

The beauty of the Rockies reminds us just how special nature is. These mighty mountains invite everyone to pause in wonder, feel the ancient history all around them, and enjoy the magic of the great outdoors.

Purple Mountain Majesties

Part of the song "America the Beautiful" is about the Rockies. Pikes Peak in Colorado inspired Katharine Lee Bates to write: "For purple mountain majesties / Above the fruited plain!"

Katharine Lee

What is the tallest mountain you've seen?

Around the World

Mountain ranges are found around the world. Let's discover what makes some of them so special!

Himalayas

Asia

This range is home to the world's highest peak, Sagarmatha (Mount Everest). It rises about 29,032 feet (8,848 meters) high.

Andes Mountains

South America

The Andes are the longest mountain range in the world. They stretch along the entire western side of South America.

Sky-High Wonder!

The height of the highest peak in the Rockies, Mt. Elbert, is roughly half the height of Sagarmatha!

Mount Kilimanjaro

Africa

This dormant volcano stands alone above the plains of Tanzania. It's famous for its snowy peak and the rare, wild animals that live nearby.

Mid-Ocean Ridge

beneath the ocean

This is the world's longest underwater mountain range. It winds across the ocean floor for more than 40,000 miles (64,374 kilometers).

Just for You

You don't have to live near the Rocky Mountains to explore their wonders. Here are some fun things to do to learn about mountains and nature at home and in your community.

National Park Search

Flip back through *Our Rocky Mountains* and see how many national parks you can find. Which one would you most like to visit?

Mountain Advertisement

Are there any mountains near where you live? Look them up online or on a map. Then, design a colorful poster to invite people to visit. What exciting sights and activities will you include?

Nature Journal

Take a walk around your neighborhood or local park. Write the names of any plants and animals you see in a nature journal. Then, compare your findings to the wildlife that lives in the Rockies. What's the same? What's different?

Ant-Sized

If you shrunk to the size of an ant and the Rockies shrunk a similar amount, how tall would the Rockies be? Work with an adult to figure it out. This will give you an idea of how you compare to the height of the Rockies!

Virtual Museum Field Trip

There are many museums throughout the Rockies—and some you can explore online! Take a virtual field trip to one of them. Discover what exhibits or videos they have and share your favorite facts with a family member or a friend.

Glossary

ecosystems—groups of living and nonliving things that make up an environment and affect each other

elevation—the height of something above sea level

erosion—the action or process of being worn away

glaciers—very large areas of ice that move slowly down slopes or valleys or over wide areas of land

hardy—able to survive outside in difficult conditions

heavy metals—dense metals that can be found in the earth, such as lead and copper

landmarks—objects or structures on land that are easy to see or recognize and may be important in history

locals—people who live in an area

northern lights—natural, colorful lights that can be seen in the sky in northern areas

remote—far away from other things

reservations—land in the United States set aside for some American Indian nations to live in and govern

resources—things found in nature that people use

sacred—highly valued or important for religious reasons

scenic—providing views of impressive natural scenery

settlers—people who move to a new area that is already populated

Index

American Indians, 8–9, 16

animals, 4–5, 8, 12, 14–15, 18, 21

Bates, Katharine Lee, 22

Continental Divide, 5

ecosystems, 14–15

erosion, 11

First Nations, 8–9, 17

formation (of the Rockies), 10–12

mining, 9, 18–19

national parks, 7, 12–13, 17

railroads, 8, 19

resources, 5, 18–19

Vinicunca, 3

Be Curious

1. Why are the Rockies so special to the First Nations?

2. What might daily life have been like for American Indians living in the Rockies long ago?

3. Why do you think settlers wanted to move into the mountains even though travel was hard?

4. How is life in the Rocky Mountains today the same or different from long ago?

About the Author

Dani Neiley grew up in Colorado and has spent countless hours in the Rocky Mountains, both in the United States and Canada. The mountains are her favorite place to be, whether it's hiking and biking on trails in the summer or snowboarding in Summit County in the winter. She lives in the foothills of Colorado, and she feels so lucky to see the Rockies every day.